diabetes
recipes

THE AUSTRALIAN
Women's Weekly

CONTENTS

AUSTRALIAN CUP AND
SPOON MEASUREMENTS
ARE METRIC.
A CONVERSION CHART
APPEARS ON PAGE 77.

All these fabulous breakfast, lunch, light
meal, main and dessert recipes are perfect
for anyone with diabetes. *Diabetes Recipes*
will bring you food that is healthy, full of
flavour and appetising – the whole family will
be happy to eat it.

Pamela Clark

Food Director

ALL ABOUT DIABETES

DISCLAIMER – The following information provides basic guidelines to healthy eating for people with diabetes. Please check with your doctor, dietitian or diabetes educator as to the suitability of this information for your diabetes management.

What is diabetes?

Diabetes is a condition in which the amount of glucose (sugar) in the blood is too high. This is because the pancreas does not make enough insulin or the insulin that it does produce is unable to do its job properly. Insulin is needed by the body to move glucose from the blood stream into the muscles and cells, to be used for energy.

There are two main types of diabetes

Type 1

Type 1 diabetes is an autoimmune disease where the body actually destroys the cells that produce insulin. So there is no insulin present. It represents 10 to 15 per cent of all cases of diabetes and normally occurs in children or young adults but can also occur in adults. While we don't know the exact cause of type 1 diabetes, it is thought that some people have a genetic predisposition for this condition and when exposed to a trigger, possibly a viral infection, the immune system then destroys the insulin-producing cells in the pancreas. Type 1 diabetes is not caused by lifestyle factors. People with type 1 diabetes require insulin injections several times a day for life.

Type 2

Type 2 diabetes occurs as a consequence of various lifestyle and genetic factors. It results in there not being enough insulin to meet the body's need or, in some cases, the insulin that is produced no longer works efficiently to move glucose from your blood into your cells (insulin resistance). Type 2 represents 85 to 90 per cent of all cases of diabetes. Lifestyle factors such as unhealthy eating and lack of physical activity can contribute to its development. Other risk factors include family history, large waist circumference ('apple' shape), being overweight, certain ethnic backgrounds and pre-diabetes. Pre-diabetes is a condition that occurs when the blood glucose level is higher than normal but not high enough to be diagnosed as diabetes.

Type 2 is the most common form of diabetes. While it usually affects adults, more young people, and even children, are being diagnosed all the time. Often symptoms of type 2 diabetes go unnoticed as the disease develops gradually. Symptoms may include blurred vision, skin infections, slow healing and tingling and numbness in the feet. Sometimes no symptoms are noticed at all.

Persistent high blood glucose (sugar) levels in either type 1 or type 2 diabetes can damage the body's organs. This damage is referred to as diabetes-related complications.

High glucose levels can affect:

Vision
Diabetic retinopathy is the leading cause of blindness in Australians aged under 60. The development of retinopathy is strongly related to the length of time diabetes has been present and the degree of blood glucose control. Regular checks and treatment can prevent blindness caused by retinopathy.

Kidney function
Your kidneys help to clean your blood. They remove waste from the blood and pass it out of the body in the urine. Over time diabetes can cause damage to the kidneys which causes them to leak. You won't notice damage to your kidneys until it's quite advanced so it is important you have your kidney function checked yearly to pick up any problems. Your kidneys are also affected by high blood pressure so that should get checked at least every three months.

Circulation and sensation to the lower limbs
Neuropathy or peripheral nerve disease and vascular damage may lead to lack of sensation, leg ulcers and serious foot problems from which lower limb amputation may result. Personal daily foot checks and thorough annual foot examinations conducted by your doctor or podiatrist will help to reduce your risk of lower limb complications.

Large blood vessels
People with diabetes are at increased risk of heart disease and stroke associated with high blood glucose levels, high blood pressure and cholesterol. High glucose levels can also increase the risk of infection, delay wound healing and increase the risk of gum disease.

While these complications are serious and can be life threatening, with appropriate lifestyle changes and attention to blood glucose control, people with diabetes can substantially reduce the risk of developing these complications.

Diabetes cannot be cured. It can however be managed by adopting a healthy lifestyle and taking tablets and/or insulin, as required. In this book we have set out to give advice on how to eat well, enjoy healthy foods and manage blood glucose levels.

People with diabetes are encouraged to follow the same healthy eating principles as the general population. This means, three evenly spread meals a day. Daily intake should consist of 4-5 servings of high-fibre breads and cereal foods, at least 5 servings of vegetables, 2-3 servings of fruit, 2-3 servings of low-fat dairy products (including milk, yogurt and cheese) 1-2 servings of lean protein (including meat, poultry, fish, legumes and nuts) and small amounts of good (unsaturated) fats.

We encourage you to increase your physical activity. Current guidelines recommend that you exercise for at least 30 minutes every day. This includes a mixture of aerobic exercises such as walking and resistance exercises such as lifting weights. It is very important to discuss any increase or change to your exercise routine with your doctor or diabetes educator.

The more low GI (Glycemic Index) carbohydrates in the meal, the greater the health benefits.

Why is GI important?
Both the quantity and quality of the carbohydrate in a food counts. The GI is a measure of carbohydrate absorption/release. Low GI foods (GI less than or equal to 55) are those carbohydrate-containing foods that have a slow rate of digestion and absorption so they do not raise your blood glucose levels too rapidly. Therefore you should select mostly foods with a low GI for your main meals and snacks.

An interesting note: the way a food is cooked can influence its GI rating. If the food is overcooked so that it is 'broken down' too much it will have a higher GI than it would in its less-processed state, eg: mashed potato has a higher GI than boiled or baked potato, and over-cooked rice or pasta will have a higher GI compared to when they are cooked al dente.

*The GI values we have given for the recipes in this book are estimates only.

Low GI – some helpful hints

Fruit, such as apples, apricots, bananas, grapefruit, grapes, kiwifruit, oranges, peaches, pears and plums, have a low GI.

Choose kumara (orange sweet potato) instead of white potato varieties.

Legumes, sweet corn and peas have a low GI.

Add lentils, barley, split peas, haricot beans and pasta pieces to soups.

Add kidney beans, borlotti beans or lentils to casseroles.

Add lentils, canned beans and even rolled oats to rissoles, in combination with the meat base.

Choose unprocessed rolled oats, oat brans, rice bran or lower-fat muesli for breakfast.

Ice-cream – look for low GI and low-fat varieties.

Jam – look for 100 per cent fruit or low GI varieties and use without butter.

Milk should be low fat or no fat.

Pasta – all varieties are low GI, but wholemeal varieties are a better choice because they have a higher fibre, vitamin and mineral content. Don't overcook pasta.

Vinegar and vinaigrette dressings can lower blood glucose levels by slowing the rate of food emptying from the stomach. Red or white wine vinegars are both good choices.

Yogurt is best bought in the low-fat variety, with no added sugar.

We provide the kilojoule content so you can stay within recommended energy intake guidelines. Daily energy intake requirements vary among individuals according to your age, body weight, level of physical activity and whether you need to lose or gain weight.

Energy (kilojoules)
Average adult's daily intake should be around 7500-8000 kilojoules.

Total fat
Daily intake should be limited to 30-35 per cent of total kilojoules; that is, 40-50g of fat per day.

Saturated fat
Saturated fat intake should be less than seven per cent of total daily kilojoule allowance; that is, less than 10g daily.

Carbohydrates
Daily intake should be 50-60 per cent of total kilojoules; that is, 200-250g per day. Use low GI, high-fibre carbohydrate sources wherever possible.

Dietary fibre
Recommendations are 28g for women and 38g for men of dietary fibre daily.

Protein
Protein intake should be 10-15 per cent of total daily kilojoules. The ideal intake should be no more than 80-100g per day. As a guideline, allow 1g of protein for each kg of your ideal body weight; ie an 80kg person should eat only 80g of protein a day.

BREKKY BERRY SMOOTHIE

prep time 5 minutes makes 1 cup (250ml)
nutritional count per serving 0.8g total fat
(0.2g saturated fat); 765kJ (183 cal);
28.7g carbohydrate; 13.1g protein; 3.3g fibre;
177mg sodium; low GI

½ cup (75g) frozen mixed berries
½ cup (125ml) chilled low-fat milk
¼ cup (70g) low-fat vanilla-flavoured yogurt
1 weet-bix (15g), crushed

1 Blend ingredients until smooth.
2 Pour into glass; serve immediately.

MANGO LASSI

prep time **10 minutes** serves 2
nutritional count per serving **3g total fat**
(1.7g saturated fat); 849kJ (203 cal);
32.6g carbohydrate; 9.6g protein; 2.3g fibre;
105mg sodium; low GI

1 medium ripe mango (430g), peeled,
   chopped coarsely
1 cup (250ml) buttermilk
⅓ cup (95g) low-fat fruit-flavoured yogurt
2 tablespoons lime juice

1 Blend ingredients until smooth.
2 Pour into glasses; serve immediately.

PORRIDGE WITH BANANA AND WALNUTS

prep + cook time **15 minutes** serves **4**
nutritional count per serving **14.2g total fat**
(4.4g saturated fat); 1517kJ (363 cal);
44.9g carbohydrate; 12.3g protein; 5.5g fibre;
92mg sodium; low GI

2 cups (500ml) water
1 cup (250ml) low-fat milk
1⅓ cups (120g) rolled oats
2 medium bananas (400g), sliced thickly
½ cup (50g) walnuts, chopped coarsely
1 tablespoon honey
1⅓ cups (330ml) low-fat milk, extra

1 Combine the water and milk in medium saucepan; bring to the boil. Reduce heat; add oats. Simmer, stirring, about 5 minutes or until porridge is thick and creamy.
2 Serve porridge topped with banana, nuts, honey and extra milk.

BIRCHER MUESLI WITH FIGS AND PISTACHIOS

prep time 15 minutes (+ refrigeration) serves 4
nutritional count per serving 16.9g total fat
(4.4g saturated fat); 1726kJ (413 cal);
46.8g carbohydrate; 14.4g protein; 8.4g fibre;
98mg sodium; low GI

1½ cups (135g) rolled oats
¼ cup (30g) oat bran
¼ cup (15g) natural bran flakes
¾ cup (180ml) low-fat milk
¾ cup (180ml) orange juice
¾ cup (200g) low-fat greek style yogurt
½ teaspoon ground cinnamon
½ cup (70g) roasted pistachios,
    chopped coarsely
1 large orange (300g), segmented
2 medium fresh figs (120g), sliced thinly

1 Combine cereals, milk, juice, yogurt and cinnamon in large bowl. Cover, refrigerate overnight. Stir in half the nuts.
2 Divide muesli among serving bowls; top with orange segments, figs and remaining nuts.

BRAN AND CRANBERRY MUESLI

prep time **10 minutes** serves **6**
nutritional count per serving **2.1g total fat
(0.4g saturated fat); 723kJ (173 cal);
28.3g carbohydrate; 7.6g protein; 6.2g fibre;
122mg sodium; low GI**

**1 cup (90g) rolled oats
¾ cup (55g) all-bran
¼ cup (35g) dried cranberries
2 cups (500ml) low-fat milk
1 large banana (230g), sliced thinly
125g (4 ounces) fresh raspberries**

1 Combine oats, bran and cranberries in small bowl to make muesli mixture.
2 Place ⅓ cup muesli in each bowl; top with milk, banana and raspberries.

BLUEBERRY HOTCAKES

prep + cook time **35 minutes** serves **6**
nutritional count per serving **2.3g total fat**
(0.7g saturated fat); 1233kJ (295 cal);
46.2g carbohydrate; 17.5g protein; 6.2g fibre;
455mg sodium; low GI

1 egg, separated
2 egg whites, extra
½ cup (125ml) apple sauce
1 teaspoon vanilla extract
3 cups (840g) low-fat yogurt
1¾ cups (280g) wholemeal self-raising flour
230g (7 ounces) fresh blueberries

1 Beat all egg whites in small bowl with electric mixer until soft peaks form.
2 Combine egg yolk, apple sauce, extract, 2 cups (560g) of the yogurt, flour and half the blueberries in large bowl; fold in egg whites, in two batches.
3 Heat oiled small frying pan; pour ¼ cup (60ml) of the batter into pan. Cook until bubbles appear on surface. Turn hotcake; cook until browned lightly. Remove from pan; cover to keep warm. Repeat with remaining batter.
4 Serve hotcakes topped with remaining yogurt and blueberries.

CHEESE AND HERB EGG-WHITE OMELETTE

prep + cook time **35 minutes** serves **4**
nutritional count per serving **3g total fat
(1.5g saturated fat); 823kJ (197 cal);
18.7g carbohydrate; 21.5g protein; 4g fibre;
389mg sodium; low GI**

**12 egg whites
4 green onions (scallions), sliced thinly
¼ cup finely chopped fresh chives
¼ cup finely chopped fresh chervil
½ cup finely chopped fresh flat-leaf parsley
⅓ cup (40g) coarsely grated reduced-fat
    cheddar cheese
⅓ cup (35g) coarsely grated reduced-fat
    mozzarella cheese
4 slices (180g) soy-linseed bread, toasted**

1 Preheat grill (broiler).
2 Beat a quarter of the egg whites in small bowl with electric mixer until soft peaks form; fold in a quarter of the combined onion and herbs.
3 Pour mixture into 20cm (8-inch) heated lightly oiled non-stick frying pan; cook, uncovered, over low heat until omelette is browned lightly underneath.
4 Sprinkle a quarter of the combined cheeses on half of the omelette. Place pan under preheated grill (broiler) until cheese begins to melt and omelette sets; fold omelette over to completely cover cheese. Carefully slide onto serving plate; cover to keep warm.
5 Repeat process three times with remaining egg white, onion and herb mixture, and cheese. Serve omelettes with toast and extra chopped herbs.

tips **If the handle of your frying pan is not heatproof, cover it with aluminium foil before placing it under the grill.**

SCRAMBLED EGGS FLORENTINE

prep + cook time **20 minutes** serves **4**
nutritional count per serving **13g total fat**
(2.7g saturated fat); 1463kJ (350 cal);
29.2g carbohydrate; 25.6g protein; 7.4g fibre;
572mg sodium; low GI

4 eggs
6 egg whites
2 tablespoons low-fat milk
2 tablespoons finely chopped fresh chives
2 teaspoons olive oil
150g (4½ ounces) baby spinach leaves
8 slices (360g) soy-linseed bread, toasted

1 Whisk eggs, egg whites, milk and chives in medium bowl. Heat oil in large frying pan, add egg mixture; cook, stirring, over low heat until creamy.
2 Place spinach in colander over sink; pour over about 2 cups of boiling water. Drain well.
3 Serve spinach and eggs with toast.

CHEESY CORN ON RYE

prep + cook time **5 minutes** serves **2**
nutritional count per serving **4.4g total fat**
(1.7g saturated fat); 1120kJ (268 cal);
42.2g carbohydrate; 10.6g protein; 7.2g fibre;
595mg sodium; low GI

310g (10 ounces) canned corn kernels,
    rinsed, drained
2 tablespoons low-fat ricotta cheese
40g (1½ ounces) baby spinach leaves
2 slices rye bread (90g), toasted

1 Heat corn in medium heatproof bowl in
microwave oven on HIGH (100%) for about
30 seconds; stir in cheese and spinach.
2 Serve toast topped with corn mixture.

BUTTERNUT PUMPKIN SOUP

prep + cook time 35 minutes (+ cooling) **serves** 4
nutritional count per serving 4.4g total fat
(0.7g saturated fat); 1559kJ (373 cal);
59.6g carbohydrate; 16.6g protein; 11.5g fibre;
377mg sodium; low GI

1 teaspoon olive oil
1 small leek (200g), sliced thinly
1 clove garlic, crushed
1 teaspoon ground cumin
½ teaspoon ground coriander
1kg (2 pounds) butternut pumpkin,
    chopped coarsely
1 large potato (300g), chopped coarsely
1 cup (250ml) salt-reduced chicken stock
3 cups (750ml) water
2 teaspoons fresh thyme leaves
8 slices (360g) soy-linseed bread, toasted

1 Heat oil in large saucepan; cook leek and
garlic, stirring, until leek is tender. Add spices;
cook, stirring, until fragrant.
2 Add pumpkin, potato, stock and the water
to pan; bring to the boil. Reduce heat; simmer,
covered, about 20 minutes or until the
vegetables are tender. Cool 10 minutes.
3 Blend or process mixture, in batches, until
smooth. Return mixture to pan; stir until hot.
Sprinkle soup with thyme; serve with toast.

LUNCHES
AND LIGHT
MEALS

ASPARAGUS FRITTATA WITH ROCKET

prep + cook time **25 minutes** serves 2
nutritional count per serving **6.3g total fat**
(1.8g saturated fat); 614kJ (147 cal);
5.4g carbohydrate; 16.3g protein; 1.9g fibre;
188mg sodium; low GI

cooking-oil spray
1 small red onion (100g), sliced thinly
170g (5½ ounces) asparagus, trimmed,
    chopped coarsely
2 eggs
2 egg whites
2 tablespoons low-fat cottage cheese
40g (1½ ounces) baby rocket (arugula) leaves
2 tablespoons lemon juice
2 teaspoons drained baby capers, rinsed

1 Preheat grill (broiler).
2 Spray small frying pan with cooking oil;
cook onion over heat, stirring, 1 minute. Add
asparagus; cook, stirring, 2 minutes.
3 Meanwhile, combine eggs, egg whites and
cheese in a medium jug. Pour over asparagus
mixture in pan. Cook, uncovered, about
5 minutes or until frittata is browned underneath.
4 Place pan under grill (broiler) for about
5 minutes or until frittata is set.
5 Combine remaining ingredients in medium
bowl; serve frittata with salad.

tips If the handle of your frying pan is not heatproof,
cover it with aluminium foil before placing it under the
grill. Frittata is delicious served warm, but if you like it
cold, and want to take it to work, make it the evening
before. Keep it in the fridge, then wrap it in plastic the
next morning.

CARROT AND LENTIL SOUP WITH CARAWAY TOASTS

prep + cook time **1 hour 10 minutes** serves **6**
nutritional count per serving **3.4g total fat**
(1.4g saturated fat); 1091kJ (261 cal);
37.8g carbohydrate; 13.7g protein; 12.6g fibre;
433mg sodium; medium GI

1 cup (250ml) salt-reduced vegetable stock
2 large brown onions (400g), chopped finely
2 cloves garlic, crushed
1 tablespoon ground cumin
6 large carrots (1kg), chopped coarsely
2 trimmed celery stalks (200g),
    chopped coarsely
1.375 litres (5½ cups) water
½ cup (100g) brown lentils
½ cup (125ml) buttermilk
caraway toasts
6 slices (270g) wholemeal bread
⅓ cup (25g) finely grated parmesan cheese
2 cloves garlic, crushed
1 teaspoon caraway seeds
2 tablespoons finely chopped fresh
    flat-leaf parsley

1 Combine ½ cup (125ml) of the stock, onion, garlic and cumin in large saucepan; cook, stirring, until onion softens. Add carrot and celery; cook, stirring, for 5 minutes. Add remaining stock and the water; bring to the boil. Reduce heat; simmer, uncovered, about 20 minutes or until vegetables are tender. Cool mixture 10 minutes.

2 Blend or process mixture, in batches, until smooth. Return mixture to pan; add lentils. Simmer, uncovered, about 20 minutes or until lentils are tender.

3 Meanwhile, make caraway toasts.

4 Remove soup from heat; stir in buttermilk. Serve with caraway toasts.

caraway toasts Preheat grill (broiler). Place bread, in single layer, on oven trays; cook under grill until browned lightly on one side. Sprinkle combined cheese, garlic, seeds and parsley over untoasted sides of bread; cook under grill until browned lightly. Cut in half.

CHICKPEA SALAD

prep time **15 minutes** serves **1**
nutritional count per serving **9.8g total fat**
(2.4g saturated fat); 1530kJ (366 cal);
47.2g carbohydrate; 16.2g protein; 13g fibre;
823mg sodium; medium GI

125g (4 ounces) canned chickpeas
(garbanzo beans), rinsed, drained
1 lebanese cucumber (130g),
chopped coarsely
½ small red onion (50g), sliced thinly
¼ cup (40g) seeded kalamata olives
⅓ cup coarsely chopped fresh
flat-leaf parsley
½ small yellow capsicum (bell pepper) (75g),
chopped coarsely
1 small egg (plum) tomato (60g), seeded,
chopped coarsely
2 tablespoons low-fat tzatziki
1 slice (45g) wholemeal bread, toasted
lemon dressing
¼ teaspoon finely grated lemon rind
1 tablespoon lemon juice
1 teaspoon olive oil
¼ teaspoon ground cumin

1 Make lemon dressing.
2 Combine chickpeas, cucumber, onion,
olives, parsley, capsicum, tomato and lemon
dressing in medium bowl.
3 Serve the salad topped with tzatziki. Serve
with toast.
lemon dressing Combine ingredients in small
bowl or jar.

TOMATO AND KUMARA BROWN RICE SALAD

prep + cook time **40 minutes** serves **4**
nutritional count per serving **3g total fat**
(0.5g saturated fat); 1287kJ (308 cal);
60.3g carbohydrate; 6.9g protein; 5g fibre;
18mg sodium; medium GI

1 cup (200g) brown long-grain rice
1 small kumara (orange sweet potato) (250g),
    chopped coarsely
250g (8 ounces) red grape tomatoes, halved
2 green onions (scallions), sliced thinly
⅓ cup firmly packed fresh small basil leaves
40g (1½ ounces) trimmed rocket
    leaves (arugula)
balsamic dressing
2 tablespoons orange juice
1 tablespoon balsamic vinegar
1 teaspoon olive oil
1 clove garlic, crushed

1 Cook rice in large saucepan of boiling water,
uncovered, about 30 minutes or until tender;
drain. Rinse under cold water; drain.
2 Meanwhile, boil, steam or microwave
kumara until tender; drain.
3 Make balsamic dressing.
4 Combine rice, kumara and dressing in large
bowl with tomato, onion, basil and rocket.
balsamic dressing Combine ingredients in
screw-top jar; shake well.

SPINACH AND CHEESE QUESADILLAS

prep + cook time **40 minutes** serves **8**
nutritional count per serving **10.4g total fat**
(3.2g saturated fat); 1170kJ (280 cal);
30.5g carbohydrate; 13.9g protein; 5.2g fibre;
465mg sodium; low GI

⅔ cup (130g) low-fat cottage cheese
100g (3 ounces) baby spinach leaves
1 medium avocado (230g), chopped finely
1 cup (200g) canned mexican-style
   beans, drained
310g (10 ounces) canned corn
   kernels, drained
2 medium tomatoes (300g), seeded,
   chopped finely
1 small red onion (100g), chopped finely
2 medium zucchini (240g), grated coarsely
16 x 15cm (6-inch) flour tortillas
1 cup (100g) coarsely grated reduced-fat
   mozzarella cheese
¼ cup loosely packed fresh coriander
   (cilantro) leaves

1 Blend or process cottage cheese and
spinach until smooth.
2 Combine avocado, beans, corn, tomato,
onion and zucchini in medium bowl.
3 Preheat grill (broiler).
4 Place eight tortillas on oven trays; spread
spinach mixture over tortillas, leaving 2cm
(¾-inch) border around edge. Spread avocado
mixture over spinach mixture; top each with
the remaining tortillas.
5 Sprinkle mozzarella over quesadilla stacks.
Cook quesadillas under grill until browned
lightly. Serve sprinkled with coriander.

tips Quesadillas are filled tortillas which are grilled or
fried and served with fresh salsa. They are best eaten
as soon as they are cool enough to handle. Serve with
grated cabbage and carrot salad tossed in a lime juice
and fresh coriander dressing.

SALMON PASTA SALAD

prep + cook time **25 minutes** serves **2**
nutritional count per serving **8.5g total fat**
(2.9g saturated fat); 1860kJ (445 cal);
56.4g carbohydrate; 32.3g protein; 5.1g fibre;
146mg sodium; low GI

1 cup (150g) spiral pasta
170g (5½ ounces) asparagus, trimmed,
    chopped coarsely
1 teaspoon finely grated lemon rind
¼ cup (60ml) lemon juice
1 clove garlic, crushed
2 tablespoons low-fat ricotta cheese
1 small red capsicum (bell pepper) (150g),
    sliced thinly
⅓ cup coarsely chopped fresh
    flat-leaf parsley
2 green onions (scallions), sliced thinly
210g (6½ ounces) canned pink salmon in
    springwater, drained, flaked

1 Cook pasta in medium saucepan of boiling
water, uncovered, until tender. Add asparagus;
cook 1 minute. Drain.
2 Meanwhile, combine rind, juice and garlic in
large bowl; add pasta, asparagus and
remaining ingredients to bowl; toss to combine.

tip **Use any pasta you like for this salad.**

TOMATO, BEAN AND PASTA SOUP

prep + cook time **30 minutes** serves **4**
nutritional count per serving **1.4g total fat**
(0.2g saturated fat); 1045kJ (250 cal);
41.8g carbohydrate; 12.1g protein; 10.6g fibre;
424mg sodium; low GI

1 large brown onion (200g), chopped finely
1 cup (250ml) salt-reduced chicken stock
3 cups (750ml) water
410g (13 ounces) canned crushed tomatoes
1 teaspoon finely chopped fresh oregano
¾ cup (135g) wholemeal pasta spirals
410g (13 ounces) canned four-bean mix,
    rinsed, drained
2 medium zucchini (240g), chopped coarsely
2 tablespoons coarsely chopped fresh
    flat-leaf parsley

1 Cook onion and 2 tablespoons of the stock
in large saucepan, stirring, until onion softens.
Add remaining stock, the water, undrained
tomatoes and oregano; bring to the boil. Add
pasta; boil, uncovered, for 10 minutes.
2 Add beans and zucchini; simmer, uncovered,
for about 5 minutes or until pasta is tender.
Serve soup sprinkled with parsley. Serve with
soy-linseed bread, if you like.

TUNA, CELERY
AND DILL SANDWICH

prep time **10 minutes** makes **2**
nutritional count per sandwich **6g total fat**
(2.2g saturated fat); 1517kJ (363 cal);
42.5g carbohydrate; 29.9g protein; 8.4g fibre;
677mg sodium; medium GI

185g (6 ounces) canned tuna in springwater,
    drained, flaked
2 trimmed celery stalks (200g),
    chopped finely
¼ small red onion (25g), chopped finely
2 tablespoons low-fat ricotta cheese
1 tablespoon coarsely chopped fresh dill
2 teaspoons rinsed, drained baby capers
20g (¾ ounce) baby spinach leaves
4 slices (180g) rye bread, toasted

1 Combine tuna, celery, onion, cheese, dill
and capers in medium bowl.
2 Sandwich spinach and tuna mixture between
bread slices.

tip If you're taking this sandwich to work, make the
filling the night before. Put it in the fridge when you
arrive at work. Toast the bread and assemble the
sandwich just before eating.

HAM, TOMATO AND ROCKET PIZZA

prep + cook time **25 minutes** makes **2**
nutritional count per pizza **8g total fat**
(3.5g saturated fat); 1559kJ (373 cal);
43.3g carbohydrate; 27.1g protein; 8.4g fibre;
841mg sodium; medium GI

2 large wholemeal pitta breads (160g)
2 tablespoons tomato paste
150g (4½ ounces) shaved salt-reduced
    lean ham
250g (8 ounces) cherry tomatoes, halved
¼ small red onion (25g), sliced thinly
⅓ cup (80g) low-fat ricotta cheese
30g (1 ounce) baby rocket (arugula) leaves
2 tablespoons finely shredded fresh basil

1 Preheat oven to 200°C/400°F.
2 Place bread on oven trays; spread with
paste. Divide ham, tomato and onion between
breads; top with dollops of cheese.
3 Bake about 10 minutes. Serve sprinkled with
rocket and basil.

CHILLI CORIANDER LAMB
AND BARLEY SALAD

prep + cook time 50 minutes (+ refrigeration) **serves** 4
nutritional count per serving 9.7g total fat
(2.6g saturated fat); 1597kJ (382 cal);
34.1g carbohydrate; 35g protein; 7.6g fibre;
122mg sodium; low GI

1 tablespoon coriander seeds, crushed lightly
½ teaspoon dried chilli flakes
2 cloves garlic, crushed
600g (1¼ pounds) lamb backstraps
1 cup (200g) pearl barley
¼ teaspoon ground turmeric
⅓ cup each loosely packed fresh mint and
    coriander (cilantro) leaves
1 small red onion (100g), chopped finely
250g (8 ounces) cherry tomatoes, halved
¼ cup (60ml) lemon juice
2 teaspoons olive oil

1 Combine seeds, chilli and garlic in medium
bowl, add lamb; toss to coat lamb in mixture.
Cover, refrigerate 30 minutes.
2 Meanwhile, cook barley in large saucepan of
boiling water, about 20 minutes or until tender;
drain. Rinse under cold water; drain.
3 Cook lamb on heated oiled grill plate (or grill
or barbecue) until cooked as desired. Cover
lamb; stand 5 minutes, then slice thickly.
4 Meanwhile, combine remaining ingredients in
large bowl, add barley; stir to combine. Serve
barley salad with lamb.

MAINS

WARM PASTA AND LAMB SALAD

prep + cook time **50 minutes (+ refrigeration)** serves **4**
nutritional count per serving **12.2g total fat**
(2.7g saturated fat); 2249kJ (538 cal);
57.9g carbohydrate; 40.2g protein; 13.3g fibre;
310mg sodium; low GI

500g (1 pound) lamb fillets
⅓ cup (80ml) lemon juice
2 tablespoons finely chopped fresh rosemary
1 tablespoon dry red wine
1 tablespoon sweet chilli sauce
1 tablespoon olive oil
1 teaspoon light brown sugar
1 clove garlic, crushed
4 medium egg (plum) tomatoes (300g),
　 quartered
350g (11 ounces) wholemeal spiral pasta
½ cup (125ml) salt-reduced beef stock
2 tablespoons coarsely chopped fresh
　 flat-leaf parsley
500g (1 pound) spinach, trimmed,
　 chopped coarsely

1 Combine lamb, juice, rosemary, wine, sauce, half the oil, sugar and garlic in medium bowl. Cover, refrigerate 2 hours.
2 Preheat oven to 180°C/350°F. Oil oven tray.
3 Place tomato in single layer on tray. Bake about 20 minutes.
4 Cook pasta in large saucepan of boiling water, until tender; drain.
5 Meanwhile, drain lamb over medium bowl; reserve marinade. Heat remaining oil in medium frying pan; cook lamb, until browned all over and cooked as desired. Cover lamb; stand 5 minutes, then slice thinly.
6 Add reserved marinade, stock and parsley to same pan; bring to the boil.
7 Combine tomato, pasta, lamb, marinade mixture and spinach in large bowl.

GRILLED PAPRIKA CHICKEN WITH RAISIN PILAF

prep + cook time **45 minutes (+ refrigeration)** serves **8**
nutritional count per serving **4.2g total fat**
(1.2g saturated fat); 2090kJ (500 cal);
71.2g carbohydrate; 42.2g protein; 1.6g fibre;
333mg sodium; medium GI

1.2kg (2½ pounds) chicken breast fillets
2 tablespoons lemon juice
3 cloves garlic, crushed
1 teaspoon sweet paprika
1 teaspoon ground cinnamon
½ teaspoon hot paprika
2 teaspoons olive oil
1 medium brown onion (150g),
**   chopped finely**
3½ cups (700g) basmati rice
1 litre (4 cups) salt-reduced chicken stock
3 cups (750ml) water
1 cup (280g) low-fat greek-style yogurt
½ cup (80g) coarsely chopped raisins
1½ cups coarsely chopped fresh
**   coriander (cilantro)**

1 Combine chicken, juice, garlic and spices in large bowl. Cover, refrigerate 2 hours.
2 Heat oil in large saucepan; cook onion, stirring, until softened. Add rice; stir to coat in onion mixture. Add stock and the water; bring to the boil. Reduce heat; simmer, covered, stirring occasionally, about 25 minutes or until rice is tender. Remove from heat; stand, covered, 5 minutes.
3 Meanwhile, cook chicken on heated oiled grill plate (or grill or barbecue), brushing with ¼ cup (70g) of the yogurt, until browned all over and cooked through. Cover chicken; stand 5 minutes, then slice thickly.
4 Stir raisins and coriander into pilaf. Serve pilaf with chicken and remaining yogurt.

tips **Serve chicken with crusty wholemeal bread rolls.**
You could stir some finely chopped and seeded
cucumber into the remaining yogurt.

TOFU AND SPINACH STIR-FRY

prep + cook time 25 minutes (+ refrigeration)
serves 4
nutritional count per serving 6.2g total fat
(1g saturated fat); 1676kJ (401 cal);
60.4g carbohydrate; 20.6g protein; 9g fibre;
626mg sodium; low GI

350g (11 ounces) firm tofu
2 tablespoons hoisin sauce
1 tablespoon oyster sauce
1 tablespoon salt-reduced soy sauce
1 teaspoon finely grated fresh ginger
2 cloves garlic, crushed
2 teaspoons peanut oil
1 large brown onion (200g), sliced thinly
1 medium red capsicum (bell pepper) (200g),
    sliced thinly
200g (6½ ounces) snow peas
350g (11 ounces) spinach, trimmed,
    chopped coarsely
¼ cup (60ml) water
350g (11 ounces) fresh egg noodles

1 Cut tofu into 2cm (¾-inch) cubes; spread, in single layer, on tray lined with absorbent paper. Cover tofu with more absorbent paper; stand 10 minutes.
2 Combine sauces, ginger, garlic and tofu in medium bowl. Cover, refrigerate for 2 hours.
3 Heat oil in wok; stir-fry onion and capsicum until onion softens. Add peas, spinach, the water and tofu mixture; stir-fry until spinach wilts.
4 Meanwhile, place noodles in large heatproof bowl, cover with boiling water; stand until tender, drain.
5 Divide noodles among serving bowls, top with tofu and vegetable mixture.

FISH AND OVEN-ROASTED CHIPS

prep + cook time 55 minutes serves 4
nutritional count per serving 7g total fat
(2.2g saturated fat); 1141kJ (273 cal);
21.4g carbohydrate; 27.7g protein;
3.7g fibre; 169mg sodium; medium GI

5 small potatoes (600g)
1 teaspoon sea salt
½ teaspoon cracked black pepper
cooking-oil spray
4 x 120g (4-ounce) firm white fish fillets
2 tablespoons rinsed, drained baby capers
1 tablespoon finely chopped fresh dill
1 teaspoon finely grated lemon rind
⅓ cup (80ml) lemon juice
1 medium lemon (140g), cut into wedges
citrus salad
1 medium orange (240g), peeled, segmented
1 lebanese cucumber (130g),
    chopped coarsely
40g (1½ ounces) each baby spinach and
    rocket (arugula) leaves
1 tablespoon white wine vinegar

1 Preheat oven to 220°C/425°F. Oil large
baking dish.
2 Halve unpeeled potatoes lengthways; cut
each half into six wedges. Combine potato,
in single layer, in dish with salt and pepper;
spray lightly with cooking-oil spray. Roast about
45 minutes or until browned lightly and tender.
3 Meanwhile, make citrus salad.
4 Cook fish in large heated oiled frying
pan until browned both sides and cooked
as desired.
5 Serve fish drizzled with combined capers,
dill, rind and juice. Serve with chips, citrus
salad and lemon wedges.
citrus salad Combine ingredients in a
medium bowl.

tip We used bream fillets in this recipe but you can use
other firm white fish, such as whiting or john dory.

CHICKEN AND PUMPKIN CURRY

prep + cook time **45 minutes** serves 2
nutritional count per serving **8.7g total fat**
(4.6g saturated fat); 1973kJ (472 cal);
58.4g carbohydrate; 32.7g protein;
8.3g fibre; 368mg sodium; medium GI

½ cup (100g) brown long-grain rice
1 small red onion (100g), chopped finely
2 tablespoons finely chopped coriander
(cilantro) root and stem mixture
¼ cup firmly packed fresh coriander
(cilantro) leaves
2 fresh long red chillies, chopped coarsely
2 cloves garlic, crushed
5cm (2-inch) piece fresh ginger (25g),
grated finely
1 teaspoon ground turmeric
1 cup (250ml) salt-reduced chicken stock
180g (5½ ounces) chicken breast fillet,
sliced thinly
¼ cup (60ml) light coconut milk
150g (4½ ounces) butternut pumpkin, cut
into 1cm (½-inch) pieces
115g (3½ ounces) baby corn,
chopped coarsely
1 cup (80g) bean sprouts
2 tablespoons fresh coriander (cilantro)
leaves, extra

1 Cook rice in large saucepan of boiling water until tender; drain.
2 Meanwhile, blend onion, coriander root and stem mixture, coriander leaves, chilli, garlic, ginger and turmeric until smooth.
3 Cook paste in medium saucepan, stirring, until fragrant. Add stock, chicken and coconut milk; bring to the boil. Reduce heat; simmer, covered, 10 minutes.
4 Add pumpkin and corn to pan; simmer, uncovered, about 10 minutes or until pumpkin is tender.
5 Serve rice topped with curry, sprouts and extra coriander.

tips Brown rice takes about 30 minutes to cook, sometimes less depending on how crunchy you like it. If you want takeaway curry, the whole recipe can be made a day ahead, then reheated in a microwave oven at lunch time.

PUMPKIN AND SPLIT PEA TAGINE

prep + cook time **55 minutes** serves **4**
nutritional count per serving **7g total fat**
(1.5g saturated fat); 1484kJ (355 cal);
55.9g carbohydrate; 19.1g protein;
11g fibre; 323mg sodium; medium GI

1 cup (200g) green split peas
1 tablespoon olive oil
1 medium brown onion (150g),
    chopped finely
2 cloves garlic, crushed
2 teaspoons ground coriander
2 teaspoons ground cumin
2 teaspoons ground ginger
1 teaspoon sweet paprika
1 teaspoon ground allspice
1kg (2 pounds) pumpkin, cut into
    3cm (1¼-inch) pieces
410g (13 ounces) canned crushed tomatoes
1 cup (250ml) water
1 cup (250ml) salt-reduced vegetable stock
2 tablespoons honey
200g (6½ ounces) green beans, trimmed,
    chopped coarsely
¼ cup coarsely chopped fresh
    coriander (cilantro)

1 Cook split peas in medium saucepan of boiling water, until tender; drain. Rinse peas under cold water; drain.
2 Meanwhile, heat oil in large saucepan; cook onion, stirring, until softened. Add garlic and spices; cook, stirring, about 2 minutes or until fragrant. Add pumpkin; stir to coat pumpkin in spice mixture.
3 Stir in undrained tomatoes, the water and stock; bring to the boil. Reduce heat; simmer, uncovered, about 20 minutes or until pumpkin is tender. Stir in honey, beans and split peas; simmer, uncovered, about 5 minutes or until beans are tender. Remove from heat; stir in coriander.

tips Traditional to North Africa, a tagine is an aromatic casserole, usually cooked and served in an earthenware dish, also called a tagine. Serve with steamed couscous.

BROWN RICE PILAF

prep + cook time **1 hour 15 minutes** serves **2**
nutritional count per serving **7.6g total fat**
(1.1g saturated fat); 1944kJ (465 cal);
80.9g carbohydrate; 12.5g protein;
10g fibre; 352mg sodium; medium GI

1 small kumara (orange sweet potato) (200g),
   chopped coarsely
cooking-oil spray
½ cup (125ml) salt-reduced vegetable stock
1 cup (250ml) water
2 teaspoons olive oil
1 medium brown onion (150g),
   chopped finely
2 cloves garlic, crushed
2 trimmed celery stalks (200g), sliced thinly
150g (4½ ounces) button mushrooms, halved
¾ cup (150g) brown medium-grain rice
1 tablespoon finely grated lemon rind
½ cup loosely packed fresh flat-leaf
   parsley leaves

1 Preheat oven to 180°C/350°F.

2 Place kumara on baking-paper-lined oven tray; spray lightly with cooking-oil spray. Roast about 25 minutes or until tender.

3 Meanwhile, place stock and the water in small saucepan; bring to the boil. Reduce heat; simmer, covered.

4 Heat oil in medium saucepan; cook onion, garlic and celery, stirring, until onion softens. Add mushrooms and rice; cook, stirring, 2 minutes. Add stock, reduce heat; simmer, covered, about 50 minutes or until stock is absorbed and rice is tender. Stir in kumara, rind and parsley.

CHICKEN, LENTIL AND SPINACH PASTA

prep + cook time **35 minutes** serves **4**
nutritional count per serving **4.6g total fat**
(0.9g saturated fat); 1777kJ (425 cal);
65.1g carbohydrate; 26.4g protein;
8.6g fibre; 418mg sodium; low GI

2 teaspoons olive oil
1 small brown onion (80g), chopped finely
2 cloves garlic, crushed
150g (4½ ounces) lean minced
   (ground) chicken
½ cup (100g) red lentils
2 cups (500ml) salt-reduced chicken stock
¾ cup (180ml) water
2 tablespoons tomato paste
250g (8 ounces) baby spinach leaves
300g (9½ ounces) shell pasta

1 Heat oil in medium saucepan; cook onion and garlic, stirring, until onion softens. Add chicken; cook, stirring, until browned. Stir in lentils, stock, the water and paste; bring to the boil. Reduce heat; simmer, uncovered, about 10 minutes or until lentils are tender. Add spinach; stir until wilted.
2 Meanwhile, cook pasta in large saucepan of boiling water, until tender; drain.
3 Combine pasta and chicken sauce in large bowl.

BEEF FAJITAS

prep + cook time **50 minutes** serves **8**
nutritional count per serving **8.8g total fat**
(3.3g saturated fat); 1258kJ (301 cal);
27.4g carbohydrate; 26.1g protein;
3.8g fibre; 337mg sodium; low GI

600g (1¼ pounds) beef rump steak
16 x 16cm (6-inch) flour tortillas
1 large red capsicum (bell pepper) (350g),
   sliced thinly
1 large green capsicum (bell pepper) (350g),
   sliced thinly
1 large yellow capsicum (bell pepper) (350g),
   sliced thinly
1 large red onion (300g), sliced thinly
3 cups finely shredded iceberg lettuce
1 cup (120g) coarsely grated reduced-fat
   cheddar cheese
fresh tomato salsa
3 medium tomatoes (450g), seeded,
   chopped finely
1 medium red onion (170g), chopped finely
1 tablespoon finely chopped drained
   jalapeño chillies
¼ cup finely chopped fresh
   coriander (cilantro)
1 tablespoon lemon juice

1 Preheat oven to 180°/350°F.
2 Make fresh tomato salsa.
3 Cook beef on heated oiled grill plate (or grill or barbecue) until cooked as desired. Cover beef; stand 10 minutes, then slice thinly.
4 Wrap tortillas in foil; heat in oven about 10 minutes or until warmed through.
5 Meanwhile, cook capsicum and onion on same grill plate, until vegetables are tender.
6 Divide beef and vegetables among tortillas. Top with lettuce, cheese and fresh tomato salsa; roll to enclose filling.
fresh tomato salsa Combine ingredients in a medium bowl.

CHILLI CON CARNE

prep + cook time **40 minutes** serves **2**
nutritional count per serving **7.8g total fat**
(2.8g saturated fat); 1563kJ (374 cal);
43.3g carbohydrate; 27.8g protein;
8g fibre; 378mg sodium; medium GI

⅓ cup (65g) brown long-grain rice
1 small brown onion (80g), chopped finely
1 clove garlic, crushed
180g (5½ ounces) lean minced (ground) beef
1 teaspoon ground cumin
1 teaspoon dried chilli flakes
410g (13 ounces) canned diced tomatoes
2 tablespoons tomato paste
½ cup (125ml) water
125g (4 ounces) canned four-bean mix,
    rinsed, drained
2 tablespoons low-fat natural yogurt
¼ cup coarsely chopped fresh
    flat-leaf parsley

1 Cook rice in medium saucepan of boiling water until tender; drain.

2 Meanwhile, heat oiled medium frying pan; cook onion and garlic, stirring, until onion softens. Add beef and spices; cook, stirring, until beef is browned.

3 Add undrained tomatoes, paste and the water; bring to the boil. Reduce heat; simmer, covered, 10 minutes. Uncover; simmer about 10 minutes or until mixture thickens slightly. Stir in beans.

4 Serve rice and chilli con carne topped with yogurt. Sprinkle with parsley.

PASTA WITH TOMATOES, ARTICHOKES AND OLIVES

prep + cook time **40 minutes** serves **4**
nutritional count per serving **6.8g total fat**
(1.9g saturated fat); 1668kJ (399 cal);
58.9g carbohydrate; 15.7g protein;
13.1g fibre; 574mg sodium; low GI

2 teaspoons olive oil
1 medium brown onion (150g),
    chopped finely
2 cloves garlic, crushed
¼ cup (60ml) dry white wine
800g (1½ pounds) canned crushed tomatoes
2 tablespoons tomato paste
⅓ cup (40g) seeded black olives
390g (12½ ounces) artichoke hearts in brine,
    drained, quartered
2 tablespoons coarsely chopped fresh basil
300g (9½ ounces) wholemeal spiral pasta
⅓ cup (25g) finely grated parmesan cheese

1 Heat oil in medium saucepan; cook onion and garlic, stirring, until onion softens. Add wine, undrained tomatoes and paste; bring to the boil. Reduce heat; simmer, uncovered, about 15 minutes or until sauce has thickened. Add olives, artichokes and basil; stir until hot.
2 Meanwhile, cook pasta in large saucepan of boiling water, until tender; drain.
3 Combine pasta and sauce in large bowl. Serve pasta topped with cheese.

CHERRY UPSIDE-DOWN CAKES

prep + cook time 40 minutes makes 12
nutritional count per cake 5.1g total fat
(0.6g saturated fat); 568kJ (136 cal);
18.6g carbohydrate; 3.8g protein;
1.4g fibre; 49mg sodium; medium GI

425g (13½ ounces) canned seeded black
   cherries, drained
2 eggs
¾ cup (150g) firmly packed light brown sugar
¾ cup (90g) ground almonds
1 teaspoon vanilla extract
⅓ cup (50g) wholemeal self-raising flour
½ cup (125ml) low-fat milk

1 Preheat oven to 180°C/350°F. Grease
12-hole (⅓-cup/80ml) muffin pan. Divide
cherries among pan holes.
2 Beat eggs and sugar in small bowl with
electric mixer until light and fluffy. Stir in ground
almonds, extract, flour and milk. Spoon the
mixture into pan holes.
3 Bake about 20 minutes. Stand 5 minutes
before turning, top-side up, onto wire rack
to cool.

DESSERTS

CITRUS SALAD

prep time **15 minutes** serves **2**
nutritional count per serving **0.7g total fat**
(0.1g saturated fat); 911kJ (218 cal);
40.6g carbohydrate; 8.9g protein;
5.4g fibre; 80mg sodium; low GI

1 medium pink grapefruit (425g), segmented
2 medium navel oranges (480g), segmented
1 lime, segmented
60g (2 ounces) strawberries, quartered
½ cup (125ml) unsweetened apple juice
¾ cup (200g) low-fat fruit-flavoured yogurt

1 Combine fruit and juice in medium bowl.
2 Serve fruit topped with yogurt.

tips If you can't find pink (or ruby) grapefruit, use
regular grapefruit. Any combination of citrus fruit is fine;
mix and match to suit your taste.

BAKED CUSTARD

prep + cook time **55 minutes** serves **6**
nutritional count per serving **5.6g total fat**
(1.8g saturated fat); 836kJ (200 cal);
23.9g carbohydrate; 14.6g protein;
0g fibre; 170mg sodium; low GI

6 eggs
1 teaspoon vanilla extract
⅓ cup (75g) caster (superfine) sugar
1 litre (4 cups) hot low-fat milk
¼ teaspoon ground nutmeg

1 Preheat oven to 160°C/325°F. Grease shallow 1.5-litre (6-cup) ovenproof dish.
2 Whisk eggs, extract and sugar in large bowl; gradually whisk in hot milk. Pour custard mixture into dish; sprinkle with nutmeg.
3 Place ovenproof dish in larger baking dish; add enough boiling water to baking dish to come halfway up side of ovenproof dish. Bake about 45 minutes or until set.

BAKED APPLES WITH BERRIES

prep + cook time **55 minutes (+ refrigeration)** serves 4
nutritional count per serving **1g total fat**
(0g saturated fat); 556kJ (133 cal);
25g carbohydrate; 3.9g protein;
4.8g fibre; 35mg sodium; low GI

2 cups (300g) frozen mixed berries
4 large apples (800g)
4 cardamom pods
½ cup (140g) yogurt
2 teaspoons honey

1 Place berries in fine sieve set over small bowl, cover; thaw in refrigerator overnight.
2 Preheat oven to 160°C/325°F.
3 Core unpeeled apples about three-quarters of the way down from stem end, making hole 4cm (1½ inches) in diameter. Use small sharp knife to score around circumference of each apple. Make small deep cut in base of each apple; insert one cardamom pod into each cut.
4 Pack three-quarters of the berries firmly into apples; place apples in small baking dish. Bake, uncovered, about 45 minutes or until apples are just tender.
5 Meanwhile, mash remaining berries with a fork in small bowl; stir in yogurt and honey.
6 Serve apples with yogurt mixture.

ALLSPICE also called pimento or jamaican pepper; tastes like a combination of nutmeg, cumin, clove and cinnamon. Available whole or ground.

BARLEY a nutritious grain used in soups and stews (often as a thickener) as well as in whisky- and beer-making. Hulled barley is the least processed form of barley and is nutritious and high in fibre. Pearl barley has had the husk discarded and has been hulled and polished, much the same as rice.

BASIL

sweet the most common type of basil; used extensively in Italian dishes and one of the main ingredients in pesto.

thai also known as horapa; different from holy basil and sweet basil in both look and taste, having smaller leaves and purplish stems. It has a slight aniseed taste and is one of the identifying flavours of Thai food.

BEETROOT also known as red beets; firm, round root vegetable.

BUCKWHEAT a herb in the same plant family as rhubarb; not a cereal so it is gluten-free. Available as flour; ground (cracked) into coarse, medium or fine granules (kasha) and used similarly to polenta; or groats, which is the whole kernel sold roasted as a cereal product.

BURGHUL also called bulghur wheat; hulled steamed wheat kernels that, once dried, are crushed into various sized grains. Used in Middle Eastern dishes such as kibbeh and tabbouleh. Is not the same as cracked wheat.

BUTTERMILK in spite of its name, buttermilk is actually low in fat,

varying between 0.6 per cent and 2.0 per cent per 100ml. Originally the term given to the slightly sour liquid left after butter was churned from cream, today it is intentionally made from no-fat or low-fat milk to which specific bacterial cultures have been added during the manufacturing process.

CAPERS the grey-green buds of a warm climate (usually Mediterranean) shrub, sold either dried and salted or pickled in a vinegar brine; tiny young ones, called baby capers, are also available both in brine or dried in salt.

CARAWAY SEEDS the small, half-moon-shaped dried seed from a member of the parsley family; adds a sharp anise flavour when used in both sweet and savoury dishes.

CHEESE

cheddar semi-hard, yellow to off-white, sharp-tasting cheese named after the village in Somerset, England in which it was originally produced. When a low-fat variety is required, we use one with no more than 20 per cent fat.

cottage fresh, white, unripened curd cheese with a grainy consistency and a fat content of 15 to 55 per cent.

cream commonly called philadelphia or philly; a soft cow's-milk cheese, its fat content ranges from 14 to 33 per cent.

goat's made from goat's milk, has an earthy, strong taste. Available in soft, crumbly and firm textures, in various shapes and sizes, and sometimes rolled in ash or herbs.

mozzarella soft, spun-curd cheese; originating in southern Italy

where it was traditionally made from buffalo's milk. Now generally made from cow's milk, mozzarella is the most popular pizza cheese because of its elasticity and low melting point when heated.

parmesan also called parmigiano; is a hard, grainy cow's milk cheese originating in the Parma region of Italy. The curd for this cheese is salted in brine for a month, then aged for up to 2 years in humid conditions. Reggiano is the best parmesan, aged for a minimum of 2 years and made only in the Italian region of Emilia-Romagna.

ricotta a soft, sweet, moist, white cow's milk cheese with a low fat content (8.5 per cent) and a slightly grainy texture. The name roughly translates as "cooked again" and refers to ricotta's manufacture from whey that is a by-product of other cheese making.

CHERVIL also known as cicily; mildly fennel-flavoured member of the parsley family with curly dark-green leaves. Available both fresh and dried but, like all herbs, is best used fresh.

CHICKPEAS also called garbanzo beans, hummus or channa; an irregularly round, sandy-coloured legume used extensively in Mediterranean, Indian and Hispanic cooking. Firm texture, even after cooking, a floury mouth-feel and robust nutty flavour; available canned or dried (reconstitute for several hours in water before use).

COCONUT

cream obtained commercially from the first pressing of the coconut flesh alone, without the addition of water; the second pressing (less rich) is sold as coconut milk. Available in cans and cartons at most supermarkets.

milk not the liquid found inside the fruit, which is called coconut juice, but the diluted liquid from the second pressing of the white flesh of a coconut (the first pressing produces coconut cream). Available in cans and cartons.

CUSTARD POWDER instant mixture used to make pouring custard; similar to North American instant pudding mix.

FENNEL also called finocchio or anise; a crunchy green vegetable slightly resembling celery that's eaten raw in salads; fried as a side; or used as an ingredient in soups and sauces.

FLOUR

buckwheat ground kernels of a herb in the same plant family as rhubarb; not a cereal so it is gluten-free.

plain also known as all-purpose; unbleached wheat flour is the best for baking; the gluten content ensures a strong dough, which produces a light result.

self-raising all-purpose plain or wholemeal flour with baking powder and salt added; make yourself with plain flour sifted with baking powder in the proportion of 1 cup flour to 2 teaspoons baking powder.

wholemeal also known as wholewheat flour; milled with the wheat germ so is higher in fibre and more nutritious than plain flour.

HORSERADISH a vegetable with edible green leaves but mainly grown for its long, pungent white root. Occasionally found fresh in specialty greengrocers and some Asian food shops, but commonly purchased in bottles at the supermarket in two forms: prepared horseradish and horseradish cream.

KUMARA the Polynesian name of an orange-fleshed sweet potato; good baked, boiled, mashed or fried, similarly to other potatoes.

LEMON GRASS also known as takrai, serai or serah. A tall, clumping, lemon-smelling and tasting, sharp-edged aromatic tropical grass; the white lower part of the stem is used, finely chopped, in much of the cooking of South-East Asia. Can be found, fresh, dried, powdered and frozen in supermarkets, greengrocers and Asian food shops.

LENTILS (red, brown, yellow) dried pulses often identified by and named after their colour. Eaten by cultures all over the world, most famously perhaps in the dhals of India. Lentils have high food value.

LETTUCE

cos also known as romaine lettuce; the traditional caesar salad lettuce. Long, with leaves ranging from dark green on the outside to almost white near the core; the leaves have a stiff centre rib giving a slight cupping effect to the leaf on either side.

iceberg a heavy, crisp, firm, round lettuce with tightly packed leaves.

mesclun pronounced *mess-kluhn*; also known as mixed greens or spring salad mix. A commercial blend of assorted young lettuce and other green leaves, including baby spinach leaves, mizuna and curly endive.

LSA a mixture of ground linseeds, sunflower seed kernels and almonds; available in health-food shops or the health-food section in supermarkets.

MARSALA a fortified Italian wine produced in the region surrounding the Sicilian city of Marsala; recognisable by its intense amber colour and complex aroma. Often used in cooking.

MIRIN a Japanese champagne-coloured cooking wine, made of glutinous rice and alcohol. It is used expressly for cooking and should not be confused with sake.

MUSHROOMS

button small, cultivated white mushrooms with a mild flavour. When a recipe in this book calls for an unspecified type of mushroom, use button.

flat large, flat mushrooms with a rich earthy flavour, ideal for filling and barbecuing. They are sometimes misnamed field mushrooms, which are wild mushrooms.

shiitake are also known as chinese black, forest or golden oak mushrooms. Although cultivated, they have the earthiness and taste of wild mushrooms. Large and meaty, they can be used as a substitute for meat in some Asian vegetarian dishes.

POLENTA also known as cornmeal; a flour-like cereal made of dried corn (maize). Also the dish made from it.

PROSCIUTTO a kind of unsmoked Italian ham; salted, air-cured and aged, it is usually eaten uncooked.

RICE

arborio small, round-grain rice well-suited to absorb a large amount of liquid; the high level of starch makes it especially suitable for risottos, giving the dish its classic creaminess.

basmati a white, fragrant long-grain rice; the grains fluff up beautifully when cooked. It should be washed several times before cooking.

long-grain elongated grains that remain separate when cooked; the most popular steaming rice in Asia.

short-grain a fat, almost round grain with a high starch content; tends to clump together when cooked.

white is hulled and polished rice, can be short- or long-grain.

RISONI small rice-shaped pasta; very similar to orzo.

ROLLED BARLEY flattened barley grain rolled into flakes; looks similar to rolled oats.

ROLLED OATS flattened oat grain rolled into flakes and traditionally used for porridge. Instant oats are also available, but use traditional oats for baking.

SAUCES

fish called *naam pla* on the label if Thai-made, *nuoc naam* if Vietnamese; the two are almost identical. Made from pulverised salted fermented fish; has a pungent smell and strong taste. Available in varying intensities so use according to your taste.

japanese soy an all-purpose low-sodium soy sauce made with more wheat content than its Chinese counterparts; fermented in barrels and aged. Possibly the best table soy and the one to choose if you only want one variety.

sweet chilli sweet, relatively mild, fairly sticky, runny bottled sauce made from red chillies, sugar, garlic and white vinegar.

teriyaki a homemade or commercially bottled sauce usually made from soy sauce, mirin, sugar, ginger and other spices; it imparts a distinctive glaze when brushed on grilled meat.

SESAME OIL made from roasted, crushed, white sesame seeds; used as a flavouring rather than a medium for cooking.

SPONGE FINGER BISCUITS also known as savoiardi, savoy biscuits or lady's fingers, they are Italian-style crisp fingers made from sponge mixture.

TOFU also known as soybean curd or bean curd; an off-white, custard-like product made from the "milk" of crushed soybeans. Comes fresh as soft or firm, and processed as fried or pressed dried sheets. Fresh tofu can be refrigerated in water (changed daily) for up to 4 days.

firm made by compressing bean curd to remove most of the water. Good used in stir-fries as it can be tossed without disintegrating. Can also be preserved in rice wine or brine.

silken not a type of tofu but reference to the manufacturing process of straining soybean liquid through silk; this denotes best quality.

soft delicate texture; does not hold its shape when overhandled. Can also be used as a dairy substitute in ice-cream or cheesecakes.

TOMATOES

bottled pasta sauce a prepared tomato-based sauce sometimes called ragu or sugo on the label; comes in varying degrees of thickness and kinds of spicing.

canned whole peeled tomatoes in natural juices; available crushed, chopped or diced, sometimes unsalted or reduced salt. Use undrained.

cherry also known as tiny tim or tom thumb tomatoes; small and round.

egg also called plum or roma, these are smallish, oval-shaped tomatoes much used in Italian cooking or salads.

paste triple-concentrated tomato puree used to flavour soups, stews, sauces and casseroles.

teardrop small yellow pear-shaped tomatoes.

TORTILLA thin, round unleavened bread originating in Mexico; can be made at home or purchased frozen, fresh or vacuum-packed. Two kinds are available, one made from wheat flour and the other from corn.

TZATZIKI Greek yogurt and cucumber dish sometimes containing mint and/or garlic.

VANILLA

bean dried, long, thin pod from a tropical golden orchid; the minuscule black seeds inside the bean are used to impart a luscious vanilla flavour in baking and desserts.

extract obtained from vanilla beans infused in water; a non-alcoholic version of essence.

YOGURT we use plain full-cream yogurt in our recipes unless specifically noted otherwise. If a recipe in this book calls for low-fat yogurt, we use one with a fat content of less than 0.2 per cent.

ZUCCHINI also known as courgette; belongs to the squash family. Flowers can be stuffed or used in salads.

CONVERSION CHART

MEASURES

One Australian metric measuring cup holds approximately 250ml, one Australian metric tablespoon holds 20ml, one Australian metric teaspoon holds 5ml.

The difference between one country's measuring cups and another's is within a 2- or 3-teaspoon variance, and will not affect your cooking results. North America, New Zealand and the United Kingdom use a 15ml tablespoon. All cup and spoon measurements are level. The most accurate way of measuring dry ingredients is to weigh them. When measuring liquids, use a clear glass or plastic jug with metric markings.

We use large eggs with an average weight of 60g.

DRY MEASURES

METRIC	IMPERIAL
15g	½oz
30g	1oz
60g	2oz
90g	3oz
125g	4oz (¼lb)
155g	5oz
185g	6oz
220g	7oz
250g	8oz (½lb)
280g	9oz
315g	10oz
345g	11oz
375g	12oz (¾lb)
410g	13oz
440g	14oz
470g	15oz
500g	16oz (1lb)
750g	24oz (1½lb)
1kg	32oz (2lb)

LIQUID MEASURES

METRIC	IMPERIAL
30ml	1 fluid oz
60ml	2 fluid oz
100ml	3 fluid oz
125ml	4 fluid oz
150ml	5 fluid oz
190ml	6 fluid oz
250ml	8 fluid oz
300ml	10 fluid oz
500ml	16 fluid oz
600ml	20 fluid oz
1000ml (1 litre)	1¾ pints

LENGTH MEASURES

METRIC	IMPERIAL
3mm	⅛in
6mm	¼in
1cm	½in
2cm	¾in
2.5cm	1in
5cm	2in
6cm	2½in
8cm	3in
10cm	4in
13cm	5in
15cm	6in
18cm	7in
20cm	8in
23cm	9in
25cm	10in
28cm	11in
30cm	12in (1ft)

OVEN TEMPERATURES

These oven temperatures are only a guide for conventional ovens.
For fan-forced ovens, check the manufacturer's manual.

	°C (CELSIUS)	°F (FAHRENHEIT)
Very slow	120	250
Slow	150	275-300
Moderately slow	160	325
Moderate	180	350-375
Moderately hot	200	400
Hot	220	425-450
Very hot	240	475

The imperial measurements used in these recipes are approximate only. Measurements for cake pans are approximate only. Using same-shaped cake pans of a similar size should not affect the outcome of your baking. We measure the inside top of the cake pan to determine sizes.

INDEX

Published in 2012 by ACP Books, Sydney

ACP Books are published by ACP Magazines Limited,
a division of Nine Entertainment Co.

54 Park St, Sydney
GPO Box 4088, Sydney, NSW 2001.

phone (+61)2 9282 8618; fax (+61)2 9126 3702

acpbooks@acpmagazines.com.au; www.acpbooks.com.au

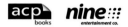

ACP BOOKS
General Manager - Christine Whiston
Editor-in-Chief - Susan Tomnay
Creative Director - Hieu Chi Nguyen
Food Director - Pamela Clark

Published and Distributed in the United Kingdom by Octopus Publishing Group
Endeavour House
189 Shaftesbury Avenue
London WC2H 8JY
United Kingdom
phone (+44)(0)207 632 5400; fax (+44)(0)207 632 5405
info@octopus-publishing.co.uk;
www.octopusbooks.co.uk

Printed by Toppan Printing Co., China

International Foreign Language Rights - Brian Cearnes, ACP Books bcearnes@acpmagazines.com.au

A catalogue record for this book is available from the British Library.
ISBN 978-1-74245-315-6